~A BINGO BOOK~

New Jersey Bingo Book

COMPLETE BINGO GAME IN A BOOK

Written By Rebecca Stark

ISBN 978-0-87386-523-4

Educational Books 'n' Bingo

Printed in the U.S.A.

NEW JERSEY BINGO DIRECTIONS

INCLUDED:

List of Terms

Templates for Additional Terms and Clues

2 Clues per Term

30 Unique Bingo Cards

Markers

1. **Either cut apart the book or make copies of ALL the sheets. You might want to make an extra copy of the clue sheets to use for introduction and review. Keep the sheets in an envelope for easy reuse.**

2. Cut apart the call cards with terms and clues.

3. Pass out one bingo card per student. There are enough for a class of 30.

4. Pass out markers. You may cut apart the markers included in this book or use any other small items of your choice.

5. Decide whether or not you will require the entire card to be filled. Requiring the entire card to be filled provides a better review. However, if you have a short time to fill, you may prefer to have them do the just the border or some other format. Tell the class before you begin what is required.

6. There are 50 terms. Read the list before you begin. If there are any terms that have not been covered in class, you may want to read to the students the term and clues before you begin.

7. There is a blank space in the middle of each card. You can instruct the students to use it as a free space or you can write in answers to cover terms not included. Of course, in this case you would create your own clues. (Templates provided.)

8. Shuffle the cards and place them in a pile. Two or three clues are provided for each term. If you plan to play the game with the same group more than once, you might want to choose a different clue for each game. If not, you may choose to use more than one clue.

9. Be sure to keep the cards you have used for the present game in a separate pile. When a student calls, "Bingo," he or she will have to verify that the correct answers are on his or her card AND that the markers were placed in response to the proper questions. Pull out the cards that are on the student's card keeping them in the order they were used in the game. Read each clue as it was given and ask the student to identify the correct answer from his or her card.

10. If the student has the correct answers on the card AND has shown that they were marked in response to the *correct questions*, then that student is the winner and the game is over. If the student does not have the correct answers on the card OR he or she marked the answers in response to *the wrong questions*, then the game continues until there is a proper winner.

11. If you want to play again, reshuffle the cards and begin again.

Have fun!

TERMS

Edwin "Buzz" Aldrin

Atlantic City

Berkeley / Carteret

Blueberry (-ies)

Border(s)

Cape May

Grover Cleveland

Coastal Plain

James Fenimore Cooper

County (-ies)

Delaware River

Thomas A. Edison

Flag

Executive Branch

Freeholders

Garden State

Highlands

Honeybee

Horse

Hudson River

Industry (-ies)

Jersey City

Jersey Shore

Judicial Branch

Knobbed Whelk

Legislature

Lenni Lenape

William Livingston

Meadowlands

Middle Atlantic States

Monmouth

Morristown

Motto

New Netherlands

New York

Newark

Paterson

William Paterson

Piedmont

Pine Barrens

Princeton

Red Oak

Ridge and Valley

Rutgers

Seal

Senator(s)

Trenton

Union

Giovanni da Verrazzano

Woodrow Wilson

New Jersey Bingo

Additional Terms

Choose as many additional terms as you would like and write them in the squares. Repeat each as desired.
Cut out the squares and randomly distribute them to the class.
Instruct the students to place their square on the center space of their card.

New Jersey Bingo

Clues for Additional Terms

Write two or three clues for each of your additional terms.

1. _____ 2. 3.	1. _____ 2. 3.
1. _____ 2. 3.	1. _____ 2. 3.
1. _____ 2. 3.	1. _____ 2. 3.

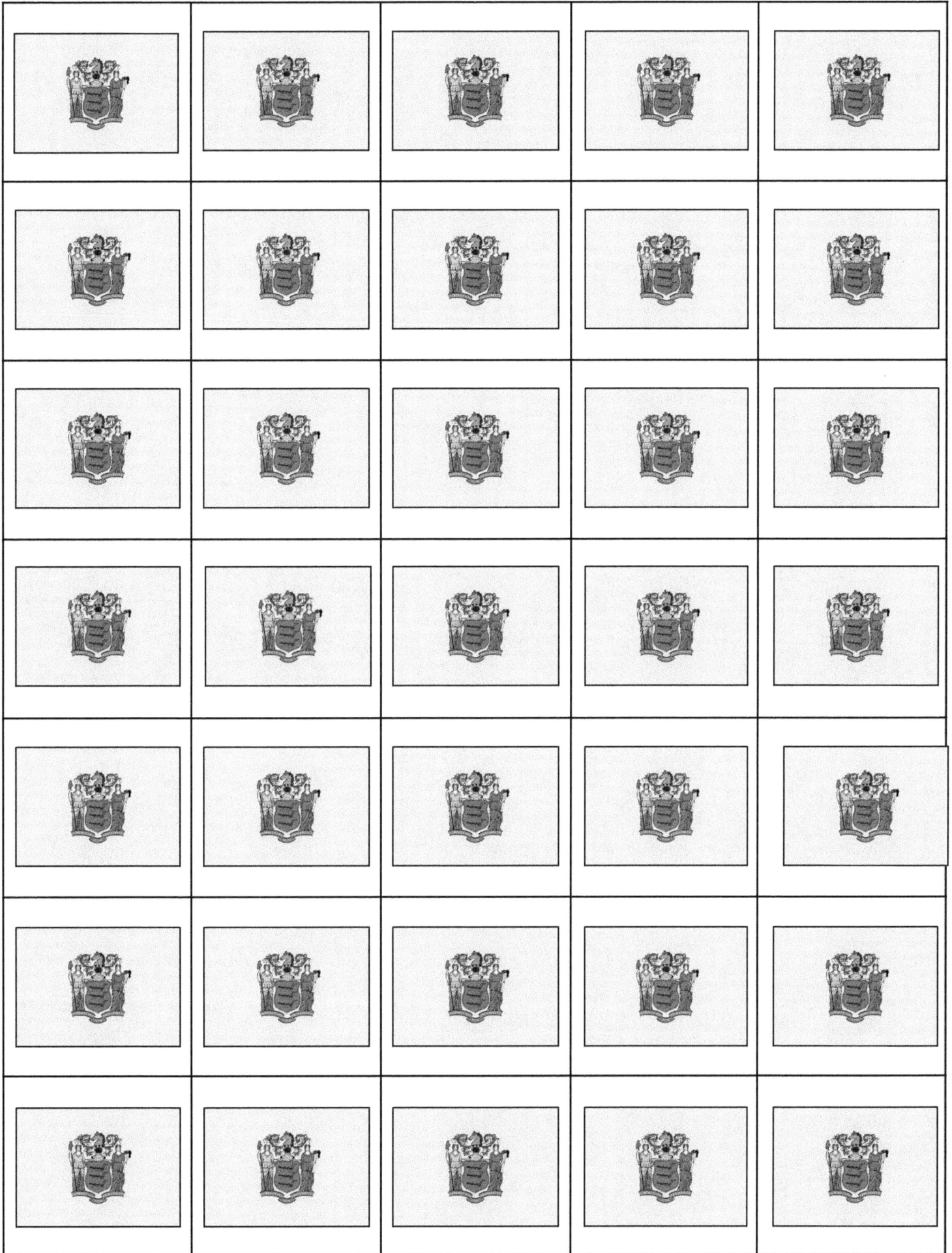

Edwin "Buzz" Aldrin 1. This astronaut was born in Montclair, New Jersey, on January 20, 1930. 2. ___ was the second human being to set foot on the moon.	**Atlantic City** 1. The board game Monopoly was based on this city. 2. Its 5.75-mile boardwalk is the longest in the world.
Berkeley / Carteret 1. When James, the Duke of York, received control of New Netherlands in 1664, he granted land to two of his friends, Lord ___ and Sir George ___. 2. Quakers eventually purchased the charters of ___ and ___ and created East and West Jersey. The two parts were joined by the British Crown in 1702.	**Blueberry (-ies)** 1. The highbush ___ became the official fruit in 2004. 2. ___ and cranberries are two important crops.
Border(s) 1. New York, Pennsylvania, and Delaware ___ New Jersey. 2. The Atlantic Ocean ___ New Jersey on the east.	**Cape May** 1. The ___ Historic District is a National Historic Landmark due to its concentration of Victorian buildings. 2. A manmade canal separates ___ from the rest of New Jersey, making it an island.
Grover Cleveland 1. This 22nd and 24th President of the United States was born in Caldwell, New Jersey. 2. He was the only President to serve two non-consecutive terms.	**Coastal Plain** 1. The southern part of the state lies in the Atlantic ___. 2. The ___ region is divided into 3 sub-provinces: the Inner Lowland along the Delaware River estuary, the Outer Lowland along the southern New Jersey shore, and the Central Upland.
James Fenimore Cooper 1. This 19th-century writer was born in Burlington, New Jersey. He is considered by many to be the first major American novelist. 2. ___ wrote *Last of the Mohicans*.	**County (-ies)** 1. The boards of chosen freeholders are the ___ legislatures. 2. The largest ___ by population is Bergen; the largest by area is Burlington.

New Jersey Bingo

Delaware River
1. The ___ forms the boundary between New Jersey and Pennsylvania and most of the boundary between New Jersey and Delaware.
2. George Washington crossed the ___ before the Battle of Trenton. The scene depicting this event is on the state quarter. It is based on an 1851 painting by Emmanuel Leutze.

Thomas A. Edison
1. The first industrial research lab was built in Menlo Park, New Jersey, for ___. The township is now named for him.
2. This inventor was nicknamed "The Wizard of Menlo Park."

Executive Branch
1. The ___ includes the governor, the lieutenant governor, the attorney general and the secretary of state and several departments.
2. The governor heads the ___.
The present-day governor is [fill in].

Flag
1. The state ___ has the state seal centered on a buff field.
2. The state ___ displays the official state colors: Jersey blue and buff.

Freeholders
1. The Board of Chosen ___ is the county government in each of the state's 21 counties.
2. ___ are equivalent to county commissioners in other states.

Garden State
1. New Jersey's nickname is the ___.
2. It is unsure how this nickname originated.

Highlands
1. The ___ lie northwest of the Piedmont. The region consists of low, rounded mountain ridges and their valleys.
2. The ___ region is actually the southern extension of the New England Upland.

Honeybee
1. The ___ is the state insect.
2. The ___ is an official state symbol in 17 states, probably because it plays such an important role in agriculture.

Horse
1. New Jersey's state animal is the ___.
2. There are many ___ farms in New Jersey. The U.S. Equestrian Team head-quarters are in Gladstone, New Jersey.

Hudson River
1. The ___ forms the boundary between New York City and the state of New Jersey.
2. The ___ is named after an English explorer who sailed for the Dutch East India Company. He explored the ___ in 1609.

New Jersey Bingo

Industry (-ies) 1. The chemical ___ is the most important ___ in New Jersey. 2. Tourism is a very important ___. The state's many resort areas along the Atlantic coastline attract many tourists.	**Jersey City** 1. Bergen was the first permanent Dutch settlement in New Jersey. It evolved into present-day ___. 2. Liberty Science Center is in Liberty State Park, which is in ___.
Jersey Shore 1. The ___ is made up of a string of barrier islands and bays. 2. Atlantic City, Asbury Park, and Wildwood are resorts along the ___.	**Judicial Branch** 1. The ___ decides how state laws should be applied. 2. The highest court in the state ___ is the Supreme Court.
Knobbed Whelk 1. The ___ is the state shell. 2. The ___ is oommonly known as the conch shell.	**Legislature** 1. The ___ makes the laws. 2. The New Jersey ___ comprises the General Assembly and the Senate. The ___ meets in the New Jersey State House in Trenton.
Lenni Lenape 1. The ___ were New Jersey's first inhabitants. They are also called the Delaware Indians because the Delaware River flowed through their lands. 2. ___ means "Real People" in the Unami language.	**William Livingston** 1. ___ was the first governor of the state of New Jersey; he served from 1776 to 1790. 2. He was governor during the American Revolution and was one of the signers of the United States Constitution in 1787.
Meadowlands 1. The ___ is a general name for the large ecosystem of wetlands in northeast New Jersey. 2. The ___ Sports Complex is a sports and entertainment complex located in East Rutherford.	**Middle Atlantic States** 1. New Jersey is one of the ___. 2. Most sources include New Jersey, New York, Pennsylvania, Delaware and Maryland in this region.

New Jersey Bingo

© Barbara M. Peller

Monmouth

1. "Molly Pitcher" is the nickname for the woman who carried water to the troops at the Battle of ___.
2. The Battle of ___ was fought on June 28, 1778. It showed the growing effectiveness of the Continental Army after its six-month encampment at Valley Forge.

Morristown

1. ___ has been called the "Military Capital of the American Revolution" because of its important role in the War for Independence.
2. The winter of 1780 was very harsh and George Washington's troops began to mutiny during their second encampment at ___.

Motto

1. "Liberty and Prosperity" is the state ___.
2. The state ___ is at the bottom of the state seal.

New Netherlands

1. The first European settlers in what is now New Jersey were Dutch, and early Colonial New Jersey was part of ___.
2. The Dutch lost ___ in 1664 when the British took control of the land.

New York

1. From 1702 to 1738 New Jersey was a British colony administered by the royal governor of ___.
2. New Jersey separated from ___ in 1738.

Newark

1. ___ is the largest city in New Jersey.
2. The sports and entertainment arena known as the Prudential Center and the New Jersey Performing Arts Center are both located in ___.

Paterson

1. ___ was the nation's first manufacturing center. It was once nicknamed Silk City.
2. This city was founded by Alexander Hamilton. The Great Falls of the Passaic River, a National Historic Landmark, is in this city.

William Paterson

1. He was the second governor of New Jersey. A city and a university are named after him.
2. He resigned as governor to become an associate justice of the U.S. Supreme Court.

Piedmont

1. This crescent-shaped plateau lies north of the Atlantic Coastal Plain. Four of the state's major rivers are in this region: the Hudson River, the Passaic River, the Ramapo River, and the Raritan River.
2. This region is only about 20 miles wide, but it includes the industrial cities of Elizabeth, Jersey City, and Newark.

Pine Barrens

1. This heavily forested area of coastal plain stretches across southern New Jersey. This area is also known as the Pinelands.
2. It was given this name because of the sandy, acidic, nutrient-poor soil that does not support the growth of crops.

New Jersey Bingo

Princeton
1. This city is famous for its University.
2. Physicist Albert Einstein lived in ___ from 1936 until his death in 1955. He often lectured at the university.

Red Oak
1. The ___ is the official state tree.
2. The ___ became the official state tree in 1950. The next year the dogwood was added as the official memorial tree.

Ridge and Valley
1. Located in the northwest corner of the state, the ___ region includes High Point, the highest point in the state at 1,803 feet.
2. The Appalachian ___ Region includes the Kittatinny Mountains and the Delaware Water Gap.

Rutgers
1. ___ is the state university.
2. The main campus of ___, the state university, is located in New Brunswick.

Seal
1. In the center of the Great ___ is a horse's head, a helmet, and three plows on a shield.
2. The two goddesses on the Great ___ represent the state motto, "Liberty and Prosperity." Liberty is on the left. Ceres, the goddess of agriculture, is on the right.

Senator(s)
1. There are 40 state ___. The term of office for a NJ state ___ is three years.
2. New Jersey's two United States ___ are [fill in] and [fill in].

Trenton
1. This city is the capital of New Jersey.
2. The Battle of ___ took place on December 26, 1776, after General Washington's crossing of the Delaware River.

Union
1. New Jersey fought on the ___ side during the Civil War.
2. New Jersey became the third state to enter the ___ on December 18, 1787, when it ratified the Constitution.

Giovanni da Verrazzano
1. This Italian explorer ___ and his crew were the first Europeans to see New Jersey.
2. ___'s ship *La Dauphine* anchored off the coast of Sandy Hook.

Woodrow Wilson
1. He was the 34th governor of New Jersey and the 28th President of the United States.
2. Before becoming governor of New Jersey, he was President of Princeton University.

New Jersey Bingo

William Paterson	Edwin "Buzz" Aldrin	Berkeley / Carteret	Horse	Border(s)
Highlands	Atlantic City	Union	Middle Atlantic States	Princeton
Trenton	Meadowlands		New York	Giovanni da Verrazzano
Senator(s)	Pine Barrens	Seal	William Livingston	Morristown
New Netherlands	Jersey City	Executive Branch	Ridge and Valley	Knobbed Whelk

New Jersey Bingo: Card No. 1

New Jersey Bingo

Senator(s)	Trenton	Judicial Branch	Piedmont	Lenni Lenape
Morristown	Freeholders	Coastal Plain	Pine Barrens	Motto
County (-ies)	Jersey City		Jersey Shore	Seal
Newark	Paterson	Meadowlands	Woodrow Wilson	Border(s)
Princeton	Union	Executive Branch	Highlands	Ridge and Valley

New Jersey Bingo

Jersey City	Seal	Freeholders	William Livingston	Trenton
Morristown	Atlantic City	James Fenimore Cooper	Edwin "Buzz" Aldrin	Industry (-ies)
Pine Barrens	Union		Motto	Blueberry (-ies)
Meadowlands	County (-ies)	New Netherlands	Newark	Judicial Branch
Ridge and Valley	Delaware River	Executive Branch	Woodrow Wilson	Lenni Lenape

New Jersey Bingo: Card No. 3

New Jersey Bingo

Meadowlands	Motto	Berkeley / Carteret	Delaware River	Lenni Lenape
Monmouth	Grover Cleveland	Edwin "Buzz" Aldrin	Piedmont	Trenton
New York	Newark		Knobbed Whelk	Horse
Seal	Atlantic City	Union	Executive Branch	Coastal Plain
Thomas A. Edison	Princeton	Cape May	Ridge and Valley	Giovanni da Verrazzano

New Jersey Bingo

Princeton	Border(s)	Pine Barrens	Coastal Plain	Delaware River
Monmouth	Seal	James Fenimore Cooper	Jersey Shore	Atlantic City
Berkeley / Carteret	Giovanni da Verrazzano		Middle Atlantic States	Hudson River
Knobbed Whelk	Lenni Lenape	William Paterson	Woodrow Wilson	Flag
Freeholders	Executive Branch	Trenton	Meadowlands	New York

New Jersey Bingo

Blueberry (-ies)	Motto	Judicial Branch	Lenni Lenape	Giovanni da Verrazzano
William Livingston	Pine Barrens	Flag	Edwin "Buzz" Aldrin	Trenton
Piedmont	Thomas A. Edison		Grover Cleveland	Jersey Shore
Executive Branch	New Netherlands	Woodrow Wilson	Cape May	Berkeley / Carteret
Morristown	Coastal Plain	William Paterson	New York	Garden State

New Jersey Bingo

William Paterson	Motto	Hudson River	Seal	Freeholders
Morristown	Lenni Lenape	Jersey City	Atlantic City	Monmouth
Giovanni da Verrazzano	Horse		Jersey Shore	Grover Cleveland
Meadowlands	Newark	James Fenimore Cooper	Senator(s)	County (-ies)
Executive Branch	Delaware River	Woodrow Wilson	Cape May	Blueberry (-ies)

New Jersey Bingo

New York	Motto	Honeybee	William Livingston	Grover Cleveland
Monmouth	Berkeley / Carteret	Piedmont	Giovanni da Verrazzano	Coastal Plain
Garden State	Delaware River		Lenni Lenape	Border(s)
Ridge and Valley	Meadowlands	Senator(s)	Thomas A. Edison	Newark
Union	Executive Branch	Cape May	Pine Barrens	Morristown

New Jersey Bingo: Card No. 8

New Jersey Bingo

Jersey Shore	Freeholders	Jersey City	Garden State	Delaware River
Thomas A. Edison	Lenni Lenape	New York	Pine Barrens	Motto
Industry (-ies)	William Paterson		Atlantic City	Honeybee
Flag	Border(s)	New Netherlands	Middle Atlantic States	Hudson River
Newark	Woodrow Wilson	James Fenimore Cooper	Senator(s)	Knobbed Whelk

New Jersey Bingo: Card No. 9

New Jersey Bingo

Senator(s)	William Livingston	Grover Cleveland	Piedmont	Garden State
Giovanni da Verrazzano	Coastal Plain	Edwin "Buzz" Aldrin	Atlantic City	Lenni Lenape
Delaware River	Motto		Horse	County (-ies)
New Netherlands	Knobbed Whelk	Flag	Woodrow Wilson	Industry (-ies)
James Fenimore Cooper	Morristown	Judicial Branch	Princeton	New York

New Jersey Bingo

Blueberry (-ies)	Motto	Pine Barrens	Flag	Morristown
Honeybee	Industry (-ies)	Middle Atlantic States	Jersey Shore	Edwin "Buzz" Aldrin
Monmouth	Lenni Lenape		Judicial Branch	Jersey City
James Fenimore Cooper	Trenton	Woodrow Wilson	Delaware River	Senator(s)
Thomas A. Edison	Executive Branch	William Paterson	Cape May	Freeholders

New Jersey Bingo

Freeholders	Border(s)	Industry (-ies)	William Livingston	Jersey Shore
Jersey City	Morristown	Berkeley / Carteret	Cape May	Atlantic City
William Paterson	Hudson River		Giovanni da Verrazzano	Piedmont
Executive Branch	Newark	Lenni Lenape	Senator(s)	Monmouth
Motto	Honeybee	Delaware River	Thomas A. Edison	Coastal Plain

New Jersey Bingo

Flag	Border(s)	Blueberry (-ies)	Industry (-ies)	Giovanni da Verrazzano
Berkeley / Carteret	Honeybee	Lenni Lenape	Jersey Shore	County (-ies)
William Livingston	Coastal Plain		Jersey City	Hudson River
New York	Woodrow Wilson	Grover Cleveland	Delaware River	Senator(s)
Executive Branch	Knobbed Whelk	Cape May	William Paterson	Middle Atlantic States

New Jersey Bingo: Card No. 13

© Barbara M. Peller

New Jersey Bingo

Highlands	Lenni Lenape	Pine Barrens	Jersey Shore	Thomas A. Edison
Coastal Plain	William Paterson	Industry (-ies)	Atlantic City	Motto
Flag	Horse		Judicial Branch	James Fenimore Cooper
Knobbed Whelk	Woodrow Wilson	Delaware River	Cleveland	Blueberry (-ies)
Executive Branch	Piedmont	County (-ies)	Morristown	New York

New Jersey Bingo

Middle Atlantic States	Jersey Shore	Pine Barrens	Freeholders	William Livingston
Blueberry (-ies)	Judicial Branch	Edwin "Buzz" Aldrin	Berkeley / Carteret	Thomas A. Edison
Giovanni da Verrazzano	William Paterson		Trenton	Motto
Executive Branch	Industry (-ies)	Honeybee	Woodrow Wilson	Flag
Morristown	Newark	Cape May	Garden State	Jersey City

New Jersey Bingo: Card No. 15

New Jersey
Bingo

Grover Cleveland	Industry (-ies)	Honeybee	Garden State	Paterson
Piedmont	County (-ies)	Hudson River	Monmouth	Horse
Flag	Border(s)		Giovanni da Verrazzano	Jersey City
Meadowlands	Coastal Plain	Executive Branch	Middle Atlantic States	Senator(s)
Thomas A. Edison	Rutgers	Cape May	Newark	Motto

New Jersey Bingo: Card No. 16

New Jersey Bingo

James Fenimore Cooper	Red Oak	Legislature	Industry (-ies)	Highlands
Middle Atlantic States	Thomas A. Edison	Woodrow Wilson	Horse	Hudson River
Jersey Shore	New York		Rutgers	Honeybee
Knobbed Whelk	Morristown	Senator(s)	Pine Barrens	County (-ies)
New Netherlands	Flag	Freeholders	William Livingston	Border(s)

New Jersey Bingo: Card No. 17

New Jersey Bingo

Garden State	Delaware River	Coastal Plain	Flag	Piedmont
Motto	James Fenimore Cooper	New Netherlands	Giovanni da Verrazzano	Thomas A. Edison
Jersey Shore	County (-ies)		Legislature	Berkeley / Carteret
Border(s)	Edwin "Buzz" Aldrin	Woodrow Wilson	Senator(s)	Judicial Branch
Rutgers	Industry (-ies)	Pine Barrens	Red Oak	Blueberry (-ies)

New Jersey Bingo

Giovanni da Verrazzano	Blueberry (-ies)	Industry (-ies)	Honeybee	Senator(s)
Middle Atlantic States	William Livingston	Motto	Freeholders	Horse
Red Oak	Delaware River		Atlantic City	Trenton
Judicial Branch	Rutgers	New Netherlands	Newark	Legislature
Berkeley / Carteret	Paterson	Morristown	New York	Cape May

New Jersey Bingo: Card No. 19

New Jersey Bingo

Highlands	Red Oak	William Livingston	Industry (-ies)	Cape May
Coastal Plain	Jersey City	Monmouth	New Netherlands	Piedmont
Border(s)	Hudson River		Meadowlands	Edwin "Buzz" Aldrin
Princeton	Union	Ridge and Valley	Newark	Rutgers
Seal	New York	Paterson	Senator(s)	Legislature

New Jersey Bingo: Card No. 20

New Jersey Bingo

Middle Atlantic States	Blueberry (-ies)	Monmouth	Industry (-ies)	Princeton
Border(s)	Legislature	Grover Cleveland	Honeybee	William Paterson
County (-ies)	Morristown		Red Oak	Pine Barrens
New Netherlands	Freeholders	Rutgers	Knobbed Whelk	New York
Meadowlands	Paterson	Cape May	James Fenimore Cooper	Newark

New Jersey Bingo

Garden State	Judicial Branch	Legislature	Berkeley / Carteret	Flag
Piedmont	William Livingston	Trenton	Honeybee	Atlantic City
Coastal Plain	Horse		William Paterson	Hudson River
Rutgers	Knobbed Whelk	Newark	Edwin "Buzz" Aldrin	Monmouth
Paterson	James Fenimore Cooper	Red Oak	County (-ies)	New Netherlands

New Jersey Bingo: Card No. 22

New Jersey Bingo

Grover Cleveland	Red Oak	Freeholders	Berkeley / Carteret	Cape May
Blueberry (-ies)	Highlands	Morristown	Middle Atlantic States	Edwin "Buzz" Aldrin
Judicial Branch	Flag		Ridge and Valley	William Paterson
County (-ies)	Paterson	Rutgers	James Fenimore Cooper	Newark
Princeton	Union	New York	New Netherlands	Legislature

New Jersey Bingo

Grover Cleveland	New York	Highlands	Red Oak	Honeybee
Legislature	Cape May	Monmouth	Piedmont	William Paterson
Hudson River	Garden State		Flag	County (-ies)
Princeton	Ridge and Valley	Rutgers	James Fenimore Cooper	Border(s)
Seal	Meadowlands	Paterson	William Livingston	Union

New Jersey Bingo

Meadowlands	Monmouth	Red Oak	Pine Barrens	Legislature
Edwin "Buzz" Aldrin	Border(s)	Middle Atlantic States	Grover Cleveland	Atlantic City
Knobbed Whelk	Honeybee		Ridge and Valley	Rutgers
Trenton	Princeton	Union	Paterson	Horse
Cape May	Highlands	Coastal Plain	Thomas A. Edison	Seal

New Jersey Bingo: Card No. 25

New Jersey Bingo

Legislature	Red Oak	Judicial Branch	Piedmont	Garden State
New Netherlands	William Livingston	Honeybee	Highlands	Grover Cleveland
Knobbed Whelk	Ridge and Valley		Horse	Meadowlands
James Fenimore Cooper	Berkeley / Carteret	Princeton	Paterson	Rutgers
Hudson River	Thomas A. Edison	Pine Barrens	Union	Seal

New Jersey Bingo

Judicial Branch	Coastal Plain	Red Oak	Highlands	Jersey City
Princeton	Ridge and Valley	Middle Atlantic States	Rutgers	Atlantic City
Woodrow Wilson	Union		Paterson	Meadowlands
Garden State	Blueberry (-ies)	Monmouth	Seal	Edwin "Buzz" Aldrin
Thomas A. Edison	Horse	Legislature	Trenton	Hudson River

New Jersey Bingo: Card No. 27

New Jersey Bingo

Judicial Branch	Highlands	Trenton	Red Oak	Grover Cleveland
Jersey City	Legislature	Ridge and Valley	Piedmont	Horse
Union	County (-ies)		Hudson River	New Netherlands
Senator(s)	Garden State	Morristown	Paterson	Rutgers
Berkeley / Carteret	Jersey Shore	Thomas A. Edison	Seal	Princeton

New Jersey Bingo

Legislature	Highlands	Garden State	Middle Atlantic States	Jersey Shore
Newark	New Netherlands	Monmouth	Hudson River	Trenton
Knobbed Whelk	Ridge and Valley		Atlantic City	Red Oak
Jersey City	Princeton	Lenni Lenape	Paterson	Rutgers
Grover Cleveland	Honeybee	Seal	Blueberry (-ies)	Union

New Jersey Bingo: Card No. 29

New Jersey Bingo

Delaware River	Red Oak	Piedmont	Jersey Shore	Rutgers
Edwin "Buzz" Aldrin	Highlands	Judicial Branch	Horse	Atlantic City
Knobbed Whelk	Flag		Hudson River	Monmouth
Seal	Blueberry (-ies)	Berkeley / Carteret	Paterson	Ridge and Valley
Princeton	Giovanni da Verrazzano	Union	Legislature	Trenton

New Jersey Bingo: Card No. 30